# Stoic Real Estate
## *Wisdom in Property Investment and Management*

# Table of Contents

# Chapter 1. Introduction

In the realm of real estate investment and management, there exists a philosophy that fuses both time-tested wisdom and modern strategy to forge success. This special report, "Stoic Real Estate: Wisdom in Property Investment and Management," explores the art of applying Stoic principles to the often unpredictable world of real estate investment, offering readers an eye-opening journey that marries philosophical wisdom to pragmatic business decisions. Our report is a vibrant blend of captivating insights, practical case studies, and strategic advice that will not only invigorate your interest but will also equip you with the tools you need to navigate the ever-changing property landscape. If you've ever entertained the idea of crafting a real estate portfolio that stands resilient through market fluctuations and yields robust profits over time, this report is a splendid resource that will inspire and guide you towards achieving that. From novices dipping their toes in the property market waters, to seasoned investors seeking a fresh perspective, prepare to be enlightened and energized by this uniquely thoughtful approach to real estate.

# Chapter 2. The Philosophical Foundation of Stoicism in Real Estate

Establishing an open conversation about the philosophical foundation of stoicism begins by revisiting our ancient origins. Stoicism, a school of Hellenistic philosophy founded in Athens by Zeno of Citium in the early 3rd century BC, has long provided guidance to humanity in dealing with life's oscillations. This school of thought emphasizes enduring pain or hardship without the display of feelings and without complaint—an ideal that perfectly suits the often rigorous cycles of the real estate market.

## 2.1. Stoicism and its Core Principles

Stoicism's core principles pivot on logic, physics, and ethics, which maybe viewed as the study of the world, the exploration of nature, and the appreciation of moral virtue respectively. These principles lead to the Stoic belief that logical comprehension of nature can lead to ethical truth. Ultimately, by understanding nature and our place within it, we can, according to the Stoics, achieve eudaimonia - a state of ultimate happiness, fulfillment, and the highest human good. This is a key element that makes Stoicism relevant in navigating real estate investment.

## 2.2. Stoicism and the Core Tenets of Real Estate Investment

Stoicism inherently emphasizes on a few critical aspects: acceptance of what one cannot control, focusing on what can be influenced, and detached observation of one's impulsive emotional responses to events. These principles can easily cross-pollinate with three core tenets of real estate: appropriate risk management, focus on controllable factors (like property maintenance and tenant management), and unwavering resilience to the inherent fluctuations of the market.

## 2.3. Practicing the Serenity Principle in Real Estate

In expanding upon the idea of recognizing what is within our control and what is not, we run into the 'Serenity Principle'. Many are familiar with its variant, the "Serenity Prayer", attributed to theologian Reinhold Niebuhr, often recited in many support group meetings. Both, however, share the same Stoic wisdom about accepting the things one cannot change, having the courage to change the things one can, and possessing the wisdom to know the difference.

In terms of real estate market challenges—like sudden market downturns, increasing interest rates, and property damage—these hurdles are largely outside of the investor's immediate control. Stoicism, in this context, advises an acceptance of these uncontrollable conditions while also issuing a challenge to real estate investors to maintain composure during distressing times.

## 2.4. Understanding Impermanence and Real Estate Cycles

Stoicism presents an understanding of the world's impermanence, teaching that change is the only constant. In the realm of real estate, this would translate to the understanding and acceptance of real estate cycles. Every long-term real estate investor should be prepared for periods of economic prosperity, slowdowns, stagnation, and even recession. These cycles are part of the nature of investing and are something that should neither be feared nor resisted but understood and planned for.

## 2.5. Emotional Resilience in Real Estate

We must remember that Stoicism doesn't advocate for an absence of emotions. Rather, it calls for a higher degree of mental fortitude to avoid being adversely affected by extreme feelings. This is instrumental in making effective real estate decisions. Emotional resilience enables investors to deal with market volatility, tenant matters, and investment decisions in a clear-headed manner, thereby helping avoid decisions that might be detrimental to their portfolio's health.

## 2.6. Investing According to Your Nature

The concept of 'living according to nature' is an essential Stoic teaching, advocating living in agreement with one's nature and, at a larger scale, the universe's nature. In real estate investment, this can be interpreted as making investment decisions that align with your inherent strengths, aptitude, financial capacity, and risk tolerance. By aligning one's investment strategy with their personal 'nature', investors can achieve genuine satisfaction and success.

By intertwining the guiding principles of Stoicism with real estate strategy, investors can forge a unique path that not only endures the tumult of real estate fluctuations but thrives amidst them. Whether confronting market volatility, making challenging decisions, or simply maintaining day-to-day property management, invoking Stoic wisdom can illuminate the path towards a flourishing real estate portfolio. This marriage between ancient wisdom and modern strategy not only opens the door to lucrative investment opportunities, but also paves the way towards a greater sense of fulfillment and contentment in one's real-estate investment journey.

# Chapter 3. Understanding the Stoic Mindset in Property Investment

Spearheading an endeavor as colossal as property investment calls for an unyielding mindset. A philosophy shaped by experience, wisdom, and a formidable spirit of resilience often holds the key. The Stoic philosophy, which has stood the test of time, offers guidelines that can be emulated in the world of real estate market.

## 3.1. The Roots of Stoic Philosophy

The Stoic philosophy is a school of Hellenistic philosophy founded by Zeno of Citium in Athens in the third century BC. Stoicism challenges individuals to focus on what they can control and respond wisely to what they cannot. Stoicism puts forth four cardinal virtues: wisdom, justice, courage, and temperance, which may be highly beneficial to a property investor's modus operandi.

## 3.2. Applying Stoic Wisdom in Property Investment

Wisdom is the ability to differentiate between what is within our control and what is not. As a property investor, discerning between these two principles is a crucial strategy. Markets will fluctuate, economic policies will change, and unexpected expenditures are bound to occur at the most inconvenient times. The wisdom lies in understanding that these elements are typically beyond your control. Instead, focus on aspects like acquisition due diligence, property maintenance, and fostering good relationships with tenants - areas that are within your control.

# 3.3. Stoic Justice in Property Investment

Stoic justice emphasizes treating other individuals in a way that reflects our principles, rather than one's position or power. For property investors, this could mean treating all stakeholders, tenants, contractors, advisors, and other property owners with fairness and respect. This approach fosters a healthier investor community and individual reputation, driving long-term growth and mutual respect.

# 3.4. Stoic Courage and Property Investment

Courage, as defined by Stoicism, is not only about facing physical challenges; rather, it is the moral courage to stand by one's decisions and face adversity. As a property investor, applying Stoic courage means making tough decisions when situations demand, sticking by them, and facing the potential consequences. It can pertain to evicting a non-paying tenant, standing by your property valuations amid criticism or venturing into a new, untested market.

# 3.5. Stoicism Demands Temperance

Temperance, as portrayed by Stoicism, describes a person's self-discipline and their ability not to overindulge in pleasures or hardships. Property investors often face situations where they must exercise temperance; for instance, avoiding rapid expansion during a market boom or refraining from panic selling during a downturn. The disciplined investor should instead strive for balanced, steady growth, in line with their risk tolerance and investment plan.

# 3.6. Embracing Stoic Mindset in Property Investment

Embracing a Stoic mindset is about more than practicing specific virtues; it requires understanding the interconnectedness of these principles and applying them collectively in your decision-making process. The successful application of this philosophy is not about a quick profit or a fast flip but about building a resilient and profitable portfolio over time.

In conclusion, Stoic philosophy can serve as a compelling framework for property investors through its emphasis on wisdom, justice, courage, and temperance. The benefits of Stoicism extend beyond the balance sheet, influencing relationships with stakeholders and shaping a more compelling, fair, courageous, disciplined investment strategy. While Stoicism cannot guarantee success in property investment, it may set resilient foundations, which can adapt and flourish regardless of the broader economic environment.

By understanding and applying the Stoic mindset, property investors can potentially steer their property portfolio to a more robust and resilient path, standing the tests of time, market fluctuations, and unprecedented challenges.

# Chapter 4. The Art of Embracing Volatility: An Insight from Stoicism

In the dynamic world of real estate investing, managing the ebbs and flows of the market is an art. Certainly, this is a field rife with volatility, yet at the same time, brimming with opportunities. The principles of Stoicism, an ancient philosophy established in the Hellenistic era, can provide a unique insight into navigating this challenging yet rewarding landscape.

## 4.1. Understanding Volatility

Volatility is a statistical measure of the dispersion of return for a given security or market index. In real estate, this can mean fluctuations in rental income, property valuation, occupancy rates, among others. Typically, higher volatility signals greater uncertainty, but also presents opportunities for higher returns.

Stoic philosophy begins with the idea of recognizing what you have control over and surrendering the things you don't. In volatile markets, this principle becomes pivotal. When faced with volatility, rather than shunning it, embrace it. Recognize that it is a part of the real estate investing world– a factor beyond your control.

## 4.2. Tools for Embracing Volatility

How do you embrace volatility in practice? Stoicism teaches us several methods.

Firstly, apply the concept of amor fati, or "love of fate". Rather than fighting market volatility, find a way to work with it, or even to love it. Here, investors must see volatility not as an obstacle, but as an opportunity. It may open doors to properties with lower prices or higher potential returns, which one could leverage for their benefit.

Secondly, the dichotomy of control should be at the forefront of your investment strategy. Differentiate between the elements you can control (like the research you carry out, or the property you choose to invest in) and those that you cannot (like market fluctuations). Then, focus your energy and efforts on what you can control.

Thirdly, remember the concept of premeditatio malorum, which is anticipating potential issues. Applied to real estate, it involves rigorous planning for potential market downturns. A contingency plan creates a buffer against sudden shifts in the market.

# 4.3. Navigating through Volatility: Real Life Examples

To better illustrate the application of stoicism in real estate investment, consider the experiences of two theoretical investors, Investor A and Investor B, during a market downturn.

Investor A reacts impulsively to the falling prices and hastily sells off properties to mitigate losses. Consequentially, they incur substantial losses, panic and regret later.

Investor B, however, having anticipated the possibility of market downturns, had an appropriate contingency plan in place. They had a diversified portfolio, reserves for sustaining costs in times of lesser rental income, and did not succumb to panic selling. Instead, they used this as an opportunity to acquire properties that were undervalued due to market fears.

The difference between their approaches lies in applying stoic principles, which clearly determined their outcomes.

# 4.4. Cultivating Emotional Resilience

Lastly, but most significant, is the development of emotional resilience. Investment is as much an emotional journey as it is a financial one. Stoics advise on cultivating apatheia, or peace of mind, which in finance means not being swayed by every market movement.

Real estate investing, especially in a volatile market, may spawn fear, stress, and even panic. The stoic way encourages mindfulness and methodical reasoning, helping you stay calm and composed during turbulent times.

Embracing volatility and leveraging it instead of fighting it, are the marks of a seasoned investor. By understanding, preparing for, and calmly managing volatility, it is possible to walk through the storm unscathed and even come out stronger on the other side.

Applying the philosophy of Stoicism can provide unexpected yet profoundly effective tools in managing real estate investments in the face of volatility. As market conditions change, remember this piece of stoic wisdom from Epictetus: "It's not what happens to you, but how you react to it that matters." Embrace volatility as an inherent part of the journey and use it as a stepping stone towards becoming a better investor and a wiser individual.

# Chapter 5. Applying Stoic Principles to Your Investment Decisions

Stoic philosophy, originating from ancient Greece and Rome, is a practical philosophy that centres on four cardinal virtues: wisdom, courage, justice, and temperance. These principles guide Stoics to live life with tranquility, effectiveness, and moral integrity. Applying these virtues in your investment decisions - studying the knowledge of markets (wisdom), taking calculated risks to gain long-term rewards (courage), treating everyone fairly and transparently (justice), and exercising restraint against immediate gratification (temperance) - can potentially lead you to financial success and personal peace.

## 5.1. The Essence of Stoic Wisdom in Investment

The Stoic philosophy espouses wisdom as a virtue, indicating an effective use of knowledge. In the investment context, wisdom results from thoroughly understanding the real estate market, its trends, your available capital, and how you want your investment portfolio to look.

A Stoic investor never stops learning, acknowledging that the real estate market is complex. Trends can shift rapidly due to a multitude of factors, such as budgetary policies, employment rates, consumer confidence, or even global pandemics. Keeping your perspective broad helps you to notice broader trends and changes in the market, enabling early response to prevent losses or capitalize on opportunities.

## 5.2. Building Courage: Embracing Risks

In Stoicism, courage goes beyond battlefield bravery. It's about acceptance of imperfections, uncertainties, and the transient nature of things. In real estate investments, a measure of risk is inevitable. It's how you prepare for and handle these risks that defines your success as an investor.

Have the courage to diversify your portfolio, venturing beyond your comfort zone. Investing in different types of properties, or even in different locations, can reduce investment risk through diversification. This approach lets you reap benefits from high-performing investments while mitigating losses from underperformers.

## 5.3. Investing with Justice: Fairness and Integrity

A Stoic doesn't see justice strictly as legal justice, but as a principle of fair dealing, truth, and integrity. As a real estate investor, maintaining fairness in your dealings creates a reputation of integrity, which is crucial in developing long-lasting relationships with buyers, sellers, renters, and other parties you interact with.

Your justice-oriented approach can manifest in practices like accurately representing property conditions, honoring lease agreements, and offering fair market prices. This attitude garners trust and respect, bringing repeat business and referrals.

# 5.4. Temperance in Real Estate: Balancing Desire and Restraint

Temperance involves balancing your desires and maintaining restraint to avoid overindulgence. In real estate investment, this relates to exercising caution and control when making decisions. For instance, auction environments can be highly charged, and it's easy to let emotions drive your decisions, potentially overbidding on a property.

The Stoic investor remains composed, maintaining focus on the long-term potential of a property rather than running astray with short-term emotions. If a property exceeds your predetermined threshold, the ability to walk away embodies the Stoic principle of temperance.

# 5.5. Case Study: Stoic Investment in Action

Examining a practical example - imagine a seasoned investor, John. John's investment strategy is based on solid market understanding, tempered by Stoic principles. His portfolio includes a mix of commercial and residential properties and his geographic diversification strategy spans both suburban and urban markets, exemplifying an application of Stoic wisdom and courage.

John's fairness in dealing with tenants and other investors has built strong professional relationships, leading to high tenant retention and referrals. His integrity in business dealings: justice, in the Stoic sense.

The economic impact of the COVID-19 pandemic made many investors panic-sell properties to cover losses. John, instead, closely studied market conditions and the trends. He demonstrated temperance, acting not out of fear, but deliberation. As a result, he purchased undervalued properties during the downturn, bolstering his portfolio for the eventual recovery.

Investing in real estate, like life, has ebbs and flows. A Stoic approach, driven by wisdom, courage, justice, and temperance, can provide an advantageous lens through which to see the market's ups and downs. This is not about eliminating risk; it's about managing it, understanding it, and using it to your advantage. In this way, Stoic philosophy, with its thousands of years behind it, can help you thrive in tomorrow's market.

# Chapter 6. Risk Management through the Lens of a Stoic Investor

The Stoics were not privy to the modern world's sophisticated investment strategies and concepts, but their wisdom remains relevant due to their profound understanding of human nature and the dynamics of life, both of which are central to the concept of risk management in real estate investing. To use the lens of Stoicism for risk management is to start with the understanding that all events in life are not entirely under our control but can be shaped and influenced to varying degrees by our actions and decisions.

## 6.1. The Dichotomy of Control

The first thing to grasp is the dichotomy of control defined by the Stoic philosopher Epictetus which states, "Some things are within our control, while others are not." Understanding this principle is the cornerstone of not just Stoic philosophy, but also successful risk management in real estate investment.

In the context of real estate, drawbacks such as unexpected fluctuations in property values, sudden market saturation, changes in tax laws, and natural disasters, fall outside an investor's control. However, investor's influence through decision-making affects other realms of the investment such as property location, type, and investment structuring, which can help mitigate certain risks. Acknowledgment of this dichotomy serves as an emotional buffer, promoting rational decision-making over reactionary responses.

# 6.2. Being Prepared

For the Stoics, preparedness was a way of life. Seneca, a famous Stoic, essentially preached risk management centuries ago, urging individuals to prepare for adversity by continually envisioning future challenges. This exercise of premeditatio malorum, or premeditation of evils, is the precursor to a modern-day risk scenario analysis and can help in assessing potential risks in your real estate investment.

Engaging in regular, detailed scenario planning allows investors to anticipate complications, calculate their impacts and formulate contingency plans. This includes assessing worst-case scenarios, like a property going unrented for an extended period, requiring significant renovation, or a drastic decrease in value due to economic factors. Preparing for these scenarios isn't pessimism, but prudence, according to the Stoics.

# 6.3. Perception of Events

The Stoic philosophers held the view that we control how we perceive events and interpret their implications. This is particularly true in real estate investment, where opportunities and threats are two sides of the same coin. Epictetus summed up this principle in his quote, "Men are disturbed not by things, but by the views which they take of them."

Economic downturns or a recession can be considered detrimental to a real estate portfolio, but they can also present opportunities for lower purchase prices, higher yields, and expansion of one's portfolio as distressed assets come to market. By shifting the perception from loss to opportunity, a Stoic investor can turn potential threats into significant gains.

# 6.4. Power of Wisdom and Prudence

In Stoic philosophy, wisdom and prudence are esteemed as cardinal virtues. Applying these virtues to real estate investing can significantly enhance risk management strategies. Wisdom, in this context, means gaining knowledge and understanding about real estate markets, different property types, financing mechanisms, tax implications, and more.

Prudence, on the other hand, encourages caution over haste. It advocates for thorough due diligence, careful portfolio diversification, and choosing quality over quantity. A real estate investor exhibiting prudence would never rush into an investment but would instead take the time to consider potential risks and rewards.

# 6.5. Emotional Resilience

Marcus Aurelius, a philosopher and Roman Emperor, believed in the virtue of emotional resilience, stating, "You have power over your mind - not outside events. Realize this, and you will find strength." The mercurial nature of real estate investment can indeed be emotionally draining and mentally challenging. Hence, resilience serves as an essential tool for weathering these storms.

By mastering emotional resilience, Stoic investors cultivate the ability to endure potential failures or setbacks, perceive them as temporary, not catastrophic, and utilize them as learning experiences. This resilience guards against irrational, fear-driven decisions and promotes clarity in navigating potential risks.

The combination of these principles forms the Stoic's approach to risk management in real estate. Through the correct use of perception, preparedness, emotional resilience and applying the dichotomy of control, real estate investors can create robust risk management strategies. Understanding that there will always be elements beyond our control, while focusing on those within control, and viewing setbacks as opportunities for growth, are central tenets that make Stoic philosophy a compelling guide for navigating the ups and downs of real estate investment.

# Chapter 7. Building Resilience in Your Real Estate Portfolio

In creating a resilient real estate portfolio, it is essential to establish a firm foundation upon the time-honored principles of risk aversion, thoughtful allocation of resources, and the measured accumulation of properties. Coupled with modern strategies for leveraging technology, market insight, and sector agility, this melding of traditional wisdom and contemporary tactics can equip any investor with the robustness needed to weather unpredictable market fluctuations and to generate substantial profits.

## 7.1. The Stoic Philosophy and Real Estate Investing

The Stoics of ancient Greece and Rome live on today through their enduring wisdom, focused as much on the pursuit of virtue as on the acceptance of the world's inherent unpredictability. Commitment to reasoned judgement, recognizing the impermanence of everything, and embracing everything in our control while accepting what is not under our control — these are the tenets of Stoicism that are deeply resonant with real estate investing.

The Stoic investor views market fluctuations not as obstacles, but as realities to be accepted. To build a resilient portfolio, one must instill a commitment to reasoned judgement, accepting the inherent risk in real estate investment while making conscious choices that limit exposure to these risks. This outlook translates into a diversified portfolio that helps minimize risk through thoughtful allocation of resources.

The Stoic approach also places a premium on wisdom, courage, justice, and self-discipline — virtues that can anchor a real estate investor in times of uncertainty and thereby foster resilience. The application of these principles in the realm of real estate investing offers both a perspective shift and a pragmatic toolset to manage risk and achieve stable long-term returns.

## 7.2. Crafting a Diversified Portfolio

Diversification represents a foundational strategy for building a resilient portfolio. It's important to diversify not just in terms of property types, but also geographically and across different sectors of the property market. This might include a mix of commercial properties, residential real estate, industrial properties, and rental properties situated in a variety of locations, both urban and rural.

By spreading investments across a range of properties, a real estate investor can protect against market changes that dramatically impact one sector or location but not others. And while diversification does not entirely eliminate risk, it certainly helps to cushion the blow of adverse market conditions.

## 7.3. Staying Agile in Market Trends

In keeping with the Stoic virtue of wisdom, success in real estate investment requires keen observation skills and a solid understanding of market trends. This includes understanding the pulse of local economies, demographic shifts, and regulatory changes.

Embracing technology can offer significant benefits in this regard. Advanced real estate software can handle large amounts of data, offering useful insights about property value trends, rental yields, vacancy rates, and other key factors. With such tools, investors can more readily identify lucrative investment opportunities and make data-driven decisions on when to buy or sell property.

However, technology should supplement, not replace, the human discernment that is integral to wise investing. After all, even the most sophisticated algorithms cannot account for every variable or predict every market shift. Despite the uncertainty — or perhaps because of this uncertainty — the Stoic investor remains steady, recognizing that the rhythm of the market is inherently unpredictable and requires ongoing attentiveness.

# 7.4. Prudent Financing and Asset Protection

One core tenet of Stoic philosophy is the acceptance of what is in our control and what is not. This applies to real estate financing and asset protection as well. It's essential to make prudent decisions based around what one can control — such as the choice of property, the financing method, and property management strategy, and accept the uncontrollable aspects such as market fluctuations.

When it comes to financing, a conservative approach is to limit the number of properties bought with borrowed money. By minimizing debt, an investor reduces exposure to financial risk and stands on more solid ground during a market downturn.

Investors must also protect their assets through insurance and a strong legal structure. The nature of real estate means that there will always be risks, such as lawsuits, natural disasters, and accidents. With the proper entity structure and comprehensive insurance coverage, a real estate investor significantly reduces their exposure to these risks.

# 7.5. Continuous Learning and Adaptation

Finally, Stoic philosophy emphasizes constant learning and self-improvement. Building a resilient real estate portfolio is an ongoing process — not a one-time task. As markets evolve and new opportunities arise, successful investors are those who are most willing to learn and adapt.

Building resilience into a real estate portfolio is not a quick fix, nor a path to overnight wealth. Rather, it is a diligent and deliberate process that merges the ancient wisdom of Stoic philosophy with the technological innovations and market strategies of modern real estate investing. By accepting the inherent uncertainty of the market, employing sound investment strategies, and focusing on continuous learning and adaptation, any real estate investor can erect a sturdy and profitable portfolio that stands the test of time.

In the face of a dynamic and sometimes tumultuous real estate market, the seasoned Stoic crafts a resilient portfolio, unshaken by volatility, and guided by time-honored principles of wisdom, courage, justice, and self-discipline. In doing so, they transform unpredictability and impermanence from potential drawbacks into objects of growth and profitability.

Crafted this way, a real estate portfolio becomes more than an assembly of properties; it is a reflection of the investor's character, brimming with Stoic virtue, mirroring resilience that withstands market fluctuation, and nurtures lasting profitability. Through this lens, the art of real estate investment reveals its profound potential to cultivate not only financial return, but also depth of character, wisdom, and resilience in its practitioner.

# Chapter 8. Stoic Wisdom for Long-term Property Investment Success

Understanding the principles of Stoicism prepares one for the long-term symbiosis with the unpredictable nature of real estate investment. The primary idea is not to allow externalities to affect your peace of mind but to understand and manage them with wisdom, forethought, and resilience.

## 8.1. Cultivating an Investor Mindset

A stoic investor understands that external events, such as market fluctuations, shouldn't dictate their peace of mind, but rather, they should focus on how they respond to these events. This response must be characterized by equanimity, resilience, and a pragmatic understanding of the market fundamentals.

One needs to develop a mindset that embraces both gains and setbacks as part and parcel of the real estate investment journey. A stoic investor opts for a long-term view, aware that there will be periods of both growth and decline. The focus remains on consistent performance, sustainable growth, and maintenance of a diversified investment portfolio that is resilient in the face of market downturns.

## 8.2. Market Cycles and Stoic Investment

A stoic investor understands that the real estate market is cyclical. Prosperity is typically followed by a downturn, which will, in turn, precede another upswing. Market trends may seem nerve-wracking, but a stoic investor rides out these cycles, armed with the knowledge that 'this too, shall pass.'

Throughout these cycles, stoic investors show resilience by sticking to their long-term investment plan. They know not to panic in the face of seemingly bleak market forecasts or over-enthusiastically jump on a trend that promises immediate wealth accumulation. They are cautious in their approach, knowing that they are not just buying properties but also tying their assets to future economic circumstances.

# 8.3. Analyzing Risk and Potential Reward

A key principle in stoicism is understanding what is within your control and what isn't. The same principle applies to risk analysis in real estate investment. There are elements within your control—like the quality and location of properties you invest in, due diligence processes, or strategic portfolio diversification. Then there are variables out of your control such as market trends, economic cycles, or regulatory changes.

Stoic investors pragmatically assess the potential risks and rewards of every investment opportunity, basing their decisions on comprehensive analysis and solid data rather than reactive emotion or speculative hype.

# 8.4. Resilience amidst Setbacks

Stoic investors understand that, like all ventures, real estate investment also comes with the possibility of setbacks. Whether it's a sudden market downturn, unexpected vacancies, or costly property repairs, setbacks are common.

Applying stoic wisdom, one does not only anticipate these challenges, but also equips oneself to handle them with resilience. It's important not to interpret setbacks as failures but as opportunities to learn, reassess, and adapt your strategies.

## 8.5. Strategic Diversification

Stoic philosophy also advises avoidance of over-exposure to a single property category or geographic location. While it might be tempting to heavily invest in what seems like a 'sure bet', stoics know the dangers of putting all eggs in one basket. They build diversified portfolios that can weather differing market scenarios and cycles, enabling gradual, steadied growth over the long term.

## 8.6. Dealing with Anxiety and Stress

Investing in real estate can often be a stress-inducing endeavor. Stoic principles counsel developing a sense of detachment towards possible outcomes. This is not to advocate apathy, but rather to foster a calm, prepared mindset that is not derailed by stress or anxiety. They know that they've made the best decisions they can with the information available, and therefore remain unflustered by unforeseen market changes.

In conclusion, the application of Stoic philosophy to real estate investment strategy is about developing a resilient mindset and a long-term approach, as well as understanding market cycles, comprehensively analyzing risks, and being prepared to tackle setbacks. This approach dramatically negates stress and aids in making sound, future-oriented investment decisions. By following these principles, you can create a real estate investment portfolio that brings forth robust profits over time, fortified against the unpredictable tides of the market.

# Chapter 9. Learning from the Stoics: When to Buy and When to Sell

Stoicism, an ancient philosophical doctrine, offers us more than wisdom for dealing with hardships. It also provides a rational framework for decision-making which can be instrumental when navigating complex fields such as real estate investment. In essence, Stoicism encourages rationality, clear judgment, and acceptance of things beyond our control. These tenets can be transformative when applied to the multifaceted and often unpredictable sector of property investment. Two major decisions, real estate buying and selling, can especially benefit from Stoic philosophy.

## 9.1. The Stoic Art of Decision-Making

Marcus Aurelius, one of the famous Stoic philosophers and Roman Emperor, believed that our actions should be driven by wisdom, justice, courage, and self-discipline. Applying this to the realm of real estate, wisdom and courage suggest thorough research and bold action when opportunities present themselves, justice prompts fair dealing, and self-discipline means maintaining a diligent strategy even in the face of market fluctuations.

When buying or selling properties, it's vital to rely on facts and logical analysis, and not be swayed by the emotional highs and lows that often plague the decision-making process in real estate. This is not to say that intuition has no place in property investment – it does, but only once it has been honed through experience and informed by comprehensive knowledge of the market.

Do thorough due diligence in every property deal. In line with the Stoic principle of self-discipline and wisdom, be vigilantly committed to understanding every facet of the property – its condition, location, potential for growth, and potential challenges.

## 9.2. Understanding the Power of Emotion

Stoics believe in understanding the role our emotions play in our decisions. In the world of real estate, most investors make common mistakes like becoming too emotionally attached to a property, falling prey to the fear of missing out (FOMO), or making reactionary decisions during market downturns. We often let our emotions take control, leading to impulsive decisions.

Marcus Aurelius wrote, "You have power over your mind - not outside events. Realize this, and you will find strength." This Stoic wisdom helps real estate investors recognize their emotional trappings and take a step back. It encourages us to evaluate our motivations and fears objectively. Are we making a decision out of anxiety? Are we holding on to a property due to attachment, even when all market analysis points to the need to sell?

## 9.3. Time to Buy: The Optimism of the Brave

*Caption: The Stoic philosopher Seneca, who believed in embracing opportunity courageously.*

The Stoic philosopher Seneca tells us that, "A gem cannot be polished without friction, nor a man perfected without trials." This Stoic insight can be applied to the choice of when to buy property. A brave investor knows that an unpopular property may well be a gem in the rough. A location that is not currently in demand can change over time, and a property that requires extensive renovations could represent a significant profit opportunity.

However, it goes without saying that one must tread cautiously and not recklessly. Always remember the Stoic emphasis on wisdom and structured thinking. It's not about taking undefined risks, but about intelligently weighing potential against risk. It's about accepting that friction - in the form of initial property conditions, location, or market status - might be part of the process, and understanding that brave, informed optimism could lead to significant rewards.

## 9.4. Time to Sell: Accepting the Inevitability of Change

On the other end of the spectrum, deciding when to sell a property also calls on the wisdom and even-mindedness championed by Stoic philosophy. A common mistake is to hold on to a property for too long, hoping for the market to reach an even higher point. However, stoics understand the inevitability and acceptance of change. Epictetus, a renowned Greek Stoic philosopher, stated, "The universe is change; our life is what our thoughts make it."

A true Stoic understands that nothing - including real estate market prices - continues ascending forever. When analysis indicates that a market peak has been touched, the Stoic investor does not allow greed to cloud their judgment. They realize that change is inevitable, hence, they sell. They balance their calculation of market trends with the understanding that change - a downturn - is probable, if not certain and thus make their move promptly.

# 9.5. Applying Dispassion and Perspective

Real estate, like life itself, is a series of decision-making under uncertain conditions. Guided by Marcus Aurelius's insight that "Everything we hear is an opinion, not a fact. Everything we see is a perspective, not the truth," we learn to view every opportunity and information piece with a lens of dispassionate rationality.

Investors should look only at the facts: location, price, condition, potential returns, and not be swayed by opinions or transient market hysteria. Crucially, they should avoid becoming emotionally entangled with their properties and instead, always maintain the viewpoint of an investor - someone who is using this purchase purely as a vehicle for financial gain.

In conclusion, when it comes to buying and selling property, Stoic wisdom serves as a potent guiding philosophy. A Stoic approach allows you to make strategic decisions, backed by intensive research and devoid of emotional influence. By practicing due diligence, understanding the power of our emotions, leveraging optimism, and accepting change, we as investors can embody the Stoic principles and allow them to guide our real estate decisions. It's worth remembering that a successful real estate journey isn't simply about understanding the markets; it's also about understanding ourselves, and there is the essence of Stoicism. It is a philosophy that goes beyond survival, aimed at thriving in any situation—whether in life or real estate investment

# Chapter 10. Strategic Planning with Stoic Principles for Property Managers

Strategic planning in property management demands not only a thorough understanding of the real estate market and financial analysis but also a well-honed ability to react to unexpected events and to steer the course of long-term commitments. Applying Stoic principles to this process can provide a unique and robust compass by which to navigate these challenges.

## 10.1. The Stoic Philosophy and Strategic Planning

Stoicism, a philosophical school that rose to prominence in Ancient Greece and Rome, prizes acceptance of what we can and cannot control, clear judgement, and emotional resilience. By adopting these foci, property managers can draft strategic plans with a thoughtful, balanced perspective.

To the Stoics, virtue, reason, and nature are closely intertwined, and understanding this relationship is key to making sound decisions. In property management, this translates to integrating ethical considerations with rational decision-making processes, carefully observing market trends, regulations, and changes in consumer behavior, and acting in harmony with these factors.

# 10.2. Stoicism and Risk Management

In property management, accurately evaluating potential risks is a cornerstone of strategic planning. Risks might consist of property market downturns, changes in zoning laws, natural disasters, or unexpected maintenance costs. Acceptance, one of Stoicism's key tenets, encourages us not to shy away from confronting these risks, but rather to face them head-on.

A Stoic property manager diminishes fear of potential adversity by practicing 'premeditatio malorum'—the premeditation of evils. This Stoic exercise involves visualizing potential negative outcomes, which can enhance a manager's capacity for strategic planning by normalizing and demystifying the concept of risk itself, thereby leading to better contingency planning.

# 10.3. Stoic Decision Making in Property Strategy

Stoicism teaches us to base decisions on reason rather than emotion. This is particularly relevant in real estate, where the markets can fluctuate quickly, often triggering rash, emotive responses. Making impulsive decisions driven by fear, greed, or excitement isn't productive. Instead, property managers should strive to remain composed under pressure, assessing situations in a measured and impartial way.

This can be achieved through 'objective representation', another Stoic practice. It encourages detachment when analyzing situations or challenges, prompting one to focus solely on facts when making decisions. When applied to property management strategy, this would involve a careful assessment of factors such as property values, market trends, and rental demand – stripped of any biases or emotional responses.

# 10.4. Embracing Change the Stoic Way

Changes are the only constant, and nowhere is this truer than in the property market. Stoicism embraces change, viewing it not as a disruption, but as an inherent part of life to be accepted and leveraged. As a property manager, interpreting the market changes, new legislation, technological incorporations, or environmental challenges through a Stoic lens could fortify strategy in ways that ensure resilience and adaptability.

# 10.5. The Virtue of Perspective in Property Management

Often, the difference between a successful property strategy and a less successful one is perspective. Stoicism counsels to see things as they are and not worst than they are, a strategy that might resonate with property managers dealing with tricky or challenging investments. This often means taking a step back, observing the bigger picture, and understanding the cyclical nature of the real estate market.

To summarize, weaving the Stoic philosophy into the stitching of property management might initially seem an eccentric weave. However, if property managers integrate these ancient Greek principles into their day-to-day operations and strategic planning, they might discover a tool of enduring, practical use. Stoicism's emphasis on facing reality, making decisions guided by reason, and accepting change harmonizes surprisingly well with the calls of a successful property strategy – equipping property managers with an adaptable, resilient mindset that could shape the future of their property portfolios.

# Chapter 11. The Stoic Path to Achieving a Balanced Real Estate Portfolio

The stoic philosophy embodies wisdom, courage, justice, and temperance in accepting and navigating through life. These virtues resonate profoundly with savvy strategies for real estate investment and management. By synthesizing stoic wisdom with real estate strategy, one can build a balanced and resilient property portfolio.

## 11.1. Embracing Uncertainty: The Heart of Real Estate Stoicism

Uncertainty is intrinsic to real estate investment. Market fluctuations, economic downturns, or unforeseen property issues can seem remarkably intimidating. However, the stoic approach suggests accepting, not fearing, these uncertainties. Stoicism teaches us that we cannot control everything that happens to us, only our reaction towards them. Therefore, embracing uncertain investment outcomes, yet remaining calm and composed, forms the heart of stoic real estate.

Staying unperturbed in the face of volatility allows investors to take calculated risks, make measured decisions, and avoid making knee-jerk reactions that might erode the value of their portfolio. A stoic investor knows not to put every egg in one basket, but rather, diversifying investments across different types of property and locations. This approach not only mitigates risks but also enhances opportunities for gain.

# 11.2. Fostering Resilience: The Backbone of a Balanced Portfolio

Resilience is a fundamental stoic virtue that aligns seamlessly with the principles of real estate investment. It encourages an attitude of perseverance and resilience, which is imperative for managing property portfolios through ups and downs. Building a resilient portfolio involves strategic planning, diligent research, and an understanding of market trends. This effort involves selecting properties that offer stable returns and withstand market shocks, thereby promoting balance in a portfolio.

Identifying resilient properties requires thorough understanding of market trends, small or large market changes, and recognizing areas with high growth potential. Moreover, investors must consider the cyclical nature of the real estate market, planning for unforeseen economic downturns. Mastering these strategies aids in constructing an adaptable and resilient real estate portfolio that reflects stoic wisdom.

# 11.3. Vigilant Due Diligence: The Guardian of Balance

Crucial to a stoic approach is the virtue of wisdom, reflected in meticulous due diligence for real estate investment. Due diligence is a comprehensive assessment that includes property inspection, valuation, legal check, rental yield calculation, and return on investment analysis. By safeguarding against potential pitfalls, it confers balance and stability to a portfolio.

Due diligence reduces the chance of making costly errors, encourages wiser investment decisions, and preserves the value of a portfolio. As a stoic investor, one mustn't let emotions disrupt diligent analysis of investment criteria. Instead, draw on wisdom and patience, displaying measured restraint where necessary, in line with the stoic principle of temperance.

## 11.4. Commitment to Continual Learning: The Lifeline of a Stoic Property Investor

Stoicism supports the pursuit of wisdom through continuous learning. This philosophy incorporates lifelong learning, constant evolution, and personal growth, which also are essential factors for the successful real estate investor. Keeping up with real estate trends, regulations, tax changes, and emerging investment opportunities is vital for maintaining a balanced portfolio.

Continual learning also promotes diversification, which is paramount to a stoic approach to investing. A balanced portfolio is a diverse portfolio, comprising a mix of various property types, like residential, commercial, or industrial, and spread across different locations. Such diversity serves to cushion the portfolio from market dips, ensuring it benefits from growth in one area while another might be declining.

## 11.5. Final Reflections: Blending Stoicsm and Real Estate

By intertwining stoic philosophy with real estate investment, we create a holistic, adaptive strategy that mitigates risk, enhances reward, and develops a balanced, resilient portfolio. Embracing uncertainty, fostering resilience, executing due diligence, and committing to continual learning constitute the cornerstones of the stoic path towards a balanced real estate portfolio.

The journey does not conclude with achieving a balanced portfolio.

Rather, the path demands continuous adaptation and evolution, growing richer with every step taken. Becoming a stoic real estate investor isn't the destination; it's about embracing the journey, the ongoing pursuit of balance, and the cultivation of wisdom in property investment and management.